Some of Our Parts

poems by

Gloria Heffernan

Finishing Line Press
Georgetown, Kentucky

Some of Our Parts

*For my mother, Margaret Cahill,
my sister, Alicia Goldberg,
and my life-long friend, Sheri Goldhirsch,
all of whom are forever part of me.*

*With love and gratitude to my husband,
Jim Heffernan
for his endless encouragement, support,
and keen editorial eye.*

Copyright © 2018 by Gloria Heffernan
ISBN 978-1-63534-465-3 First Edition
All rights reserved under International and Pan-American Copyright Conventions. No part of this book may be reproduced in any manner whatsoever without written permission from the publisher, except in the case of brief quotations embodied in critical articles and reviews.

ACKNOWLEDGMENTS

The following poems received first publication in the cited journals:

"Some of Our Parts," *CNY Branch of American Pen Women*
"I Think of Irma," *Evening Street*
"My Father's Daughter," *Pleiades*
"She Weeps for Camelot," *Evening Street*
"Sailing," *Southword*
"The Girls of Paris," *The Columbia Review*
"Taking Her Vitals," *Blood and Thunder*
"My Sister's Glasses," *The Healing Muse*
"Kaddish for My Sister," *Evening Street*
"Reunion," *Falling Star Review*
"The Family We Choose," *The Louisville Review*
"Let Morning Come," *The Healing Muse*

Publisher: Leah Maines
Editor: Christen Kincaid
Cover Art: Gloria Heffernan
Author Photo: James M. Heffernan
Cover Design: Kate Anderson, http://www.kagraphicdesign.com/

Printed in the USA on acid-free paper.
Order online: www.finishinglinepress.com
    also available on amazon.com

Author inquiries and mail orders:
Finishing Line Press
P. O. Box 1626
Georgetown, Kentucky 40324
U. S. A.

Table of Contents

Some of Our Parts 1
I Think of Irma 2
My Father's Daughter 3
She Weeps for Camelot 5
The Girls of Paris 6
Sailing 8
Goulash 9
Sentimental Journey 10
Evening in Paris 12
Scent Memory 13
Memorial Day 15
All Through the Night 16
Tea Ceremony 18
World's Fair 1964 19
Double Exposure 21
Witness 22
Cursive 23
Taking Her Vitals 24
Kaddish for My Sister 25
My Sister's Glasses 26
Reunion 27
The Family We Choose 28
Folding the Sheets 29
Let Morning Come 30
Long Distance 31
Heirloom 32
What I Want 33
Wisdom Quilt 35

Some of Our Parts

I believe in Frida Kahlo's moustache
Eleanor Roosevelt's buck teeth
Maya Angelou's wrinkled forehead

I believe in the small round wart
nested in the crease between my mother's
nose and left cheek.

I believe in my sister's thinning hair,
my best friend's gapped teeth,
my stretch marks and thick waist.

I believe that some of our parts
are no match for the sum of our parts,
and I believe the sum of our parts
is holy indeed.

I Think of Irma

On days like this,
I think of Irma—
how she brought
the breakfast tray
to my mother's room
in the hospice,
how she always knocked
before entering
and spoke to my mother
as she came and went.

I think of her light blue scrubs
pressed and creased,
the scent of laundry detergent
mixed with Dial soap
perfuming the air
after she had gone.

I remember how
every Monday morning,
her sneakers were polished white
and gleamed like new snow.

I think of her voice,
clear and tender as she greeted
my mother who seldom stirred
at her comings and goings.

I think of Irma
when I watch the news
and wonder how much
more suffering
this planet can take.
I think of her constant care
when I want to give up.

I think of her
and then I press my clothes
and polish my shoes
and go about this business
of living.

My Father's Daughter
> *The Earth is your mother, say the Native Peoples. But I say no.*
> *The Earth is my father.*

The Earth is the plot of land
where they buried the stranger
whose blood flows through my veins.
A garden of sorts,
marked with a stone,
and hidden by an overgrown Juniper bush.

The Earth is my father,
and his dreams fill my memory,
coloring the fabric of my mother's stories
that clothed me
on my journey west to the place
where his imagination
took root in my heart.

"You are your father's daughter"
she would say,
while I stared at the television
drinking in what little bits of his dreams I could claim
through borrowed images of
cowboys and Indians
and John Wayne swaggering into a saloon
with God and country on his side.

I am your daughter,
I say to the Earth.
You have carried me to the place you dreamed of
on Sunday nights while you watched Bonanza
after tucking in the child who
would never remember your touch.

It was you who made me turn my back
on that damp and crowded grave
where you are said to be at rest.

Exhumed from the place where you are buried,
you are with me now,
seeing through my eyes the images you dreamed of
long ago.

Not cowboys or Indians, or shootouts at the OK Corral,
but juniper trees, tall and graceful,
sweeping against the clouds,
and the silent explosion of color in a desert sunrise,
and your daughter standing at peace in the midst of it all,
remembering you.

She Weeps for Camelot

Stepping out in front of his mother,
he raises his hand in salute.
Already so poised
before the cameras.
It is his birthday today.
He is three years old.
Camelot's youngest prince
bidding his father farewell.

My mother watches weeping.
Her three-year-old son sleeps
on the couch by her side
while she remembers the funeral
ten months earlier
when the wind whipped
the veil that covered her face
as they handed her the tri-fold flag.

The First Lady holds
her daughter's hand
as my mother holds mine.
Silence envelopes the nation
like the black veil that covers
the young widow's face.
Even the November wind is still
as she stares ahead, a study in dignity.

Jersey City is not Camelot,
and my mother no American royalty.
But watching the flag-draped casket
roll past the Cathedral steps
she sees only a widow and her children,
and grieves for a shattered family
as her three year old son
stirs in his sleep.

The Girls of Paris

No matter their age,
they were always *the girls*,
dressed in starched white uniforms,
and white rubber-soled shoes.
They might have been nurses
lined up at the bus stop after closing time,
if not for their black aprons
dusty with powdered sugar.

The girls have blisters on their feet,
running back and forth
behind the counter all day,
and blisters on their hands
breaking the red and white string
spooling from the ceiling
for the cardboard boxes
embossed with a gold Eiffel Tower.

"Take a number, please."
The line spills out the door
on Sunday mornings
when church bells ring over Jersey City,
and the girls brace themselves
for the wave of saints and sinners
descending on the bakery
after the final hymn is sung.

"Six apple turnovers,"
orders the lady in the blue felt hat.
"Gimme a pound cake, and a babka,"
bellows the man in the pinstriped suit,
snapping his pocket watch for effect.
"Birthday cake pick up—
No, it's Cathy with a C, dammit.
Can't you read?"

She flips the sign in the window
from Come-in-We're-Open
to Sorry-We're-Closed,
and scrapes the crumbs
from the heavy trays
to scrub for tomorrow's rush.

The girls get their pick of anything
left at the end of the day.
They stock up on cheese Danish
and apple crumb cake.
She picks up her box
tied with red and white string.
Butter cookies tonight.
The kids will be happy.

Sailing

A dead roach floats on the surface
of my mother's afternoon coffee.
She watches its compatriots
scale the wall above the stove
as if they know she cannot
douse them with Raid
while dinner is cooking.
She doesn't know if roaches laugh,
but she imagines they do on days like this
when all the scrubbing in the world

seems to be for naught.
She dumps the coffee down the drain
and wipes her hands
on the green housecoat she wears
to hang out the window
clipping freshly laundered sheets to the clothesline,
watching them snap and billow in the wind
like the graceful sails of a schooner
she wishes she could board with her children
and sail away to someplace clean.

Goulash

She called it goulash
because she liked the word.
Stew lacked music.
Goulash called up
images of gypsies
strumming mandolins
under a full moon.
For me the name
only conjured images
of the rubber boots
I buckled over my shoes
on rainy days.
But when she lifted the lid
to let the aroma lure us to the table,
moonbeams filled the kitchen
and in each spoonful,
the taste of music.

Sentimental Journey

It was her favorite song.
Whenever she heard it,
she was there
on the deck
with a thousand soldiers
waving their caps
at Lady Liberty.

Gonna take a sentimental journey.
It was his song.
The song that told him
he was home.
The song that brought him
back to her.

Never thought my heart could be so yearny.
Every time it played
on the oldies station
in the kitchen
while she peeled potatoes
or pressed a meatloaf into the pan,
she would cock her head to one side,
pause and say,

*That's the song they played
on the ship
when your father came home
from the war.*

Every time she told the story,
it was both old and new,
Doris Day's voice piercing the static
of the loudspeakers,
the rumble of the engines
as the ship glided into
New York harbor.

Long to hear that 'all aboard.'
Singing along softly, swaying her hips
ever so slightly.
The closest my mother ever came to dancing.
And every time she heard it,
it brought her home.

Evening in Paris

Her favorite shade of blue
a cobalt teardrop
crowned in pleated silver cap
evoking the Eiffel Tower
at midnight

Evening in Paris
born in 1928
just like my mother
awash in jasmine and bergamot
dabbed on each pulse point

She saves the empty bottles
to perfume her lingerie drawer
and scent the hankie
she carries in her purse
to wipe our dripping noses

Ninety-nine cents
at the Five and Ten
and me with a dollar
in my pocket
on Christmas Eve

The new bottle swaddled
in its satin lined box
centered on her dresser
next to the Jean Nate
and Jergens Lotion
waiting for a special occasion

Scent Memory

I thought that was just
what men smelled like,
Big Jack, Uncle Pete, Ray the super.
I didn't know it was a blend
of whiskey, beer, sweat, and Old Spice.
It was the smell of absence,
the smell of the empty space
once occupied by my father
who liked to stop at the White Owl Tavern
now and then
for a quick Boiler Maker
and a few laughs with the guys.

When Uncle Pete came by after dinner
neat in his blue uniform,
service revolver holstered at his waist,
my mother bit her lip
remembering her stepfather roaring

up the street singing "The Old Rugged Cross,"
a sure bet it would be a long night
laced with threats and taunting
with the gun he stored
in a box in the hall closet.

I didn't know that the pigeon-toed man
lurching into the kitchen
with a paper bag under one arm was drunk
as he swept Eddie and me
into a Pabst-Blue-Ribbon hug.
He was just loud and funny,
squeezing into one of the child-sized rockers
my mother had bought on lay-away
that first Christmas after my father died.

Quietly watchful,
she extended a chilly hospitality
to her late husband's brother.
Eager to avoid a fight,
she gently corralled us
to the far corner of the kitchen,
while he held court from his pint-sized perch,
until she told him not to open the bag
when he demanded a glass.

His dark brows knit together.
"If that's the way you want it," he said,
listing to his full six feet
with the tiny wooden rocker
clinging to his rear end like a child
who refused to let go.

Eddie and I pealed with laughter
as he wriggled his hips,
unaware of the mounting tension
as he struggled to free himself
without falling face first
onto the black and white linoleum,
until he finally shoved the handles
and flung the chair to the floor.

She followed him to the door,
warning him never to return
with whiskey on his breath
and a gun at his hip.

Then she silently walked
back to the kitchen,
righted the rocking chair
and tried to silence
"The Old Rugged Cross,"
echoing through her brain.

Memorial Day

The only sign of Memorial Day in Manhattan is
the abundance of empty tables at the diner on 8th Street
where Ella Fitzgerald croons about that
old black magic called love.

I remember Memorial Day at Holy Name Cemetery,
my father's grave decorated with a wreath and a flag.
At four years old I don't know that a half century hence
I will sit in a red vinyl booth in Greenwich Village
listening to Tony Bennett
(who has picked up where Ella left off)
remembering my mother's green and yellow trowel
purchased for the sole purpose of planting flowers at the grave,
and the hedge clippers to trim the juniper bush
that nearly covers the name on the granite stone.

I am too young to know a day will come
when I won't remember his voice,
and I won't even remember having forgotten it.
But that's a long way off.
For now he still echoes in my memory
as my brother and I bicker about which one of us will
dig the hole to plant the azalea
in the only garden we have ever known.

And now Frank Sinatra is inviting me
to come fly, come fly away.
But I am earthbound,
remembering the smell of soil and grass
and the juniper scented breeze,
and my mother's hand cupped over mine,
teaching me how to hold the trowel and turn the topsoil,
and press the plant into the shallow bowl of earth.

And here on 8th Street,
Louis Armstrong has the world on a string.

All Through the Night

> *Sleep, my child, And peace attend thee*
> *All through the night...*

The fan hums softly on the night table,
its quiet song muffles
Johnny Carson's monologue
in the next room
where my mother submits
to another sleepless night.
The soft electric breeze
pulls a plume of cigarette smoke
through the doorway,
scenting my room
with Salem 100's
and Jean Naté.

The gentle whir rescues me
from the silence
where my too vivid imagination
ponders the finer points of death.
But *where is* Daddy?
But *what is* heaven?
She doesn't know how to answer
a four-year old ruminating on mortality,
so offers as substitute
an amber-eyed Jesus
enthroned in ornate brass frame
complete with nightlight
and plastic roses.

Enveloped in the white noise,
Jesus watches from his perch
on the chest of drawers
while my mother kneels
beside me teaching me to pray.
If I die before I wake...

I stumble over the words,
race to the amen,
and practice holding my breath
to fool death if it should sneak
in through the fire escape.

The fan hums its tuneless melody
all through the night—
a lullaby of sorts
while I watch the shadows from the TV
flicker across the wall,
listen to the muffled laughter
and the blare of Doc's trumpet—
anything to resist the threat of slumber.

Tea Ceremony

Steam rises from the mug
where my mother steeps the tea bag,
adds a generous splash of milk,
a heaping spoonful of sugar.

She pours the water
into my favorite blue cup
filling it only part-way,
teaching me early to see the cup
as half-full,
(and less likely to spill).

Now I drink it without sugar,
and the milk is virtuously fat free,
but still, the steam rises like a memory—
my mother in the kitchen,
the smell of toast,
the sacred quiet after
the kettle's shrill call.

World's Fair 1965

The Unisphere hovers like a ghost,
behind a misty chorus line of fountains
at the Flushing Meadow Fair Ground
where my mother is determined to
show us the whole world
in one summer day.

This is the furthest she will ever venture
from our apartment in Jersey City,
shepharding us onto the bus from
Duncan Avenue to Port Authority
And the Number 7 train to the last stop in Queens
where General Electric's City of the Future
unfurls itself at our feet.

Here among the crowded exhibit halls
and overpriced souvenir stands,
she delivers the thundering drumbeats of the Serengeti
where African tribesmen
dance to a relentless rhythm
in a booth made of palm fronds
and animal skins.

And in the Vatican Pavilion
we file past the Pieta,
where luminous marble maps the
intersection of love and agony,
and what I can't understand of the statue
I sense in my mother's reverence
at the sight of it.

Susie looks through the lens
of the old Kodak Instamatic
trying to coax Eddie into the frame.
Even at five, he wants to go his own way,
tugging crankily at our mother's hand
while she urges him to smile for the camera.

"I'm smilin' Ma...I'm smilin'" he growls
like a miniature Jimmy Cagney
while I gaze distractedly at the Disney pavilion
humming another chorus of
"It's a Small World After All."

Double Exposure

Forty years later
they hold the framed photo
taken when they were four and five years old.
She in a blue jumper,
straight hair curled into stiff coils
after sleeping in pink foam rollers all night.
He in a blue polo shirt
pressed neatly for the occasion.
Their father's blue eyes blending with
their mother's pug nose.

The long forgotten picture
reprinted and framed,
a Christmas gift from their
mother's granddaughter
who insists they pose with it now,
a testament to enduring smiles
etched into faces so resembling her own.
She poses them in a mirror image of the original,
her father on the left, her aunt on the right,
the children they were
still present in the middle-aged faces that fill the lens.
She urges them to smile

just as their mother urged them
when the Sears photographer
came to the tenement apartment
setting up his lights and tripod
to capture the smiles
that proved they would be all right
even as they tried to understand
why their father's heart attacked him.

Now her granddaughter
frames the same image
focuses on the same faces,
shoots as all say "Cheese,"
insisting on the enduring smiles
that prove they will be all right,
even on this first Christmas
without her grandmother.

Witness

My mother died
a year before the Towers fell.
I imagine how she would have
sat by the television watching bodies
rain down from the sky.
How she would have rocked
back and forth
on the edge of the bed,
her left leg shaking as her foot
tapped out a frantic SOS,
waiting to hear that I was safe,
hands trembling,
inhaling cigarette smoke,
exhaling prayers,
remembering FDR's voice
telling a grieving nation of a day
that would live in infamy.

Cursive

Her right hand,
twice the size of mine,
envelopes my left.

Pencil sharpened
and vertical,
she leads the dance
across the sky blue
lines on the page.

First the *G*,
lines and loops,
uphill and down,
like the first bike ride
with training wheels.

Her hand steers mine.
Now the graceful
Glide up into the
Elegant oval of *l*.
Down again
for the squat round *o*.

My sister teaches me
to write my name.
After ten practice runs
with her strong hand
holding on to guide and balance,
she removes the training wheels
and pushes me off.

I grip the pencil,
pedal slowly, methodically.
There it is—
my hand, my name,

my sister launching me
onto the page.

Taking Her Vitals

I carry the ICU
in the bottom of my purse
like a forgotten thumb tack
that pierces my finger
every time I reach in to find my keys.
It's always 2:00 a.m.
the night nurse taking her vitals
as if they were spare parts
to be carried away one at a time,
inexorably dismantling respiration
pulse, oxygen level, blood pressure,
urine output, bilirubin count—
clinical words intersecting
in a crossword puzzle
where Across and Down hold clues
with no answers
and the medically-induced coma
robs us of her days.
No, she is not Bed 4,
she is my sister.
I dwell in the chrome-legged chair
with the yellow plastic seat
beside her bed
hypnotized by the rhythm
of machines that blink and beep and buzz,
taking her vitals as she sleeps.

Kaddish for My Sister
*(In Memory of Alicia Cahill Goldberg
July 22, 1949—July 3, 2002)*

The seven days of mourning have passed.
We have walked around the block,
dismantled the shiva boxes,
taken the covers off the mirrors.

I look at my reflection,
searching for the image
so many have found there
        —your face—

All I see now
are the swollen eyes and puffy cheeks
that bear witness to a week of tears
as my fingers drift automatically to the
gold cross at my throat,
a gift from you two Christmases ago.

All I see now
are the dirt and stones
raining down on your casket
as the Rabbi translates patiently,
letting me know when to say Amen.

All I see now
is a plate of glass reflecting a face
I hardly recognize.
I drop the sheet back over the mirror.
There is nothing there that I need to see.
The mirror I looked to all my life
is gone.

My Sister's Glasses

My sister's trifocals
are zipped into
a quilted pouch
in my top dresser drawer
between the silk scarves
and the pantyhose.

Glaucoma had
chewed at the edges of
her eyesight,
like a rat devouring
still living prey.
Encroaching darkness

never dimmed her light.
Just one more obstacle
in a lifetime of
obstacles overcome
or overlooked.

I have saved them
since that morning
over a decade ago
when I collected
her belongings
from the ICU

as if they might
somehow be the lens
through which
I could see the world
once more
through her eyes.

Reunion

Thirty years since their last embrace,
she readies herself for their date,
choosing the red lipstick she usually
bypasses in favor of a sensible neutral.

They danced to the Bee Gees and she was
"More than a Woman"
in high heels and a swirling skirt,
beads circling the hem like tiny constellations
glittering above the dance floor.

His girls are in college now.
He shows her their pictures over salad.
"Beautiful," she says,
noticing how their dark eyes resemble his.
The entrée is seasoned with details about the divorce.
He was always so good at parting friends.
"We just grew apart," he says.

She nods sympathetically,
remembering the poem she wrote about him
for the college literary magazine.
She wonders if he kept a copy
in a box of mementoes stored on a high shelf
in the house in the 'burbs.

For dessert, they order just one slice
of strawberry cheesecake with two forks.
He dabs a speck of sweet crimson sauce
from her chin and licks it off his finger.

She no longer needs to be more than a woman.
Still, she is glad she opted for the V-neck sweater
as his eyes rest on her collarbones,
and he signals the waiter for the check.

The Family We Choose

Every room overflows with your presence—
a strand of pearls for my twenty-first birthday,
the Celtic Cross you embroidered for my fiftieth,
the tool box you gave me one Christmas,
filled with all I might ever need for home repair—
"Because every woman should know how
to use a power drill."

        When the phone rings at 2:00 a.m.,
        I know the calls you didn't return last night
        were portents of more than a night on the town.
        The doctor calls looking for next of kin.
        After forty years, we are kin indeed.
        "I suggest you come right away,"
        she advises, clinical voice steeped in calm.

At eighteen, we dubbed ourselves
best friends.
Time made us sisters.
"We are the family we choose," you said
when we celebrated birthdays and mourned losses,
welcomed each new generation,
laughed and cried without a word.

        Now in the ICU,
        where I stroked your forehead
        as you surrendered your last breath,
        the machines have gone eerily quiet.
        Lights on monitors that blinked
        only moments ago are dark and still.
        There is nothing left to fix.

The family we chose is shattered.
Your toolbox is suddenly empty
having finally faced the one thing
you could not repair—
not even with your safety goggles
and power drill.

Folding the Sheets

My mother taught me
how to tuck in the corners
of the fitted sheets,
first lengthwise
and then across,
laying the flat rectangle
on the kitchen table,
smoothing it with both hands,
and then folding it in thirds
and thirds again.
Like wrapping a present,
she would say,
as we moved on to the pillowcases
and towels.

Your bed was stripped
before I arrived.
Sheets had been
peeled off the mattress,
wadded into a ball,
stuffed into the incinerator.
Someone's thoughtful attempt
to restore order.

I pull a fitted sheet
from the hall closet.
The wrinkled ball of cotton
still bears your frustration
with the geometry
of domesticity.
I unroll it and smooth it down
over the four corners of your bed.

I will sleep here tonight
on your wrinkled sheet,
and in the morning,
fluff the pillows
and straighten your quilt
as if such gestures matter,
or ever did.

Let Morning Come
(after Jane Kenyon's "Let Evening Come")

Let the darkness of the long night
recede from the city's rooftops, blending
morning with mourning as the sun rises.

Let the taxis barrel down the streets
as if there were somewhere to go beyond
this hospital room. Let morning come.

Let the unopened envelopes pile up
in the mailbox. Let sunlight pour into
your kitchen where dishes still litter the sink.

Let pictures in their frames recall happier days.
Let the neighbors wonder about the woman
taken away in an ambulance. Let morning come.

To the milk carton in the refrigerator, to the blinking
light on the answering machine, to the ones
left behind, let morning come.

Let cold wind blow, as it will, and don't
be afraid. Grief is the outer fabric of a coat
lined with gratitude, so let mourning come.

Long Distance

It happened again,
even now,
two years after that night
when the phone rang
at 2:00 in the morning
and I knew
before I picked up
the receiver
that you were dead.

It still happens whenever
I write a poem
that I know you would love,
a reflex honed over
forty years of friendship
that compels me
to pick up the phone
and read it to you.

Heirloom

The quilt Beth made for me
is casually folded
over the arm of the couch
as if it weren't a work of art
but simply a blanket
meant to warm me
while I read a book
or sip my coffee.

Over a year in the making,
its creation spanned
two Christmases and a birthday,
in the sewing room
where her machine
overlooks the garden
that inspired the floral squares
she stitched together
into a cascade of burgundy rosettes
and pink geraniums.

It will outlive me
like the quilts of pioneer women
stitched over a century ago
hanging on museum walls
as if made only to be seen.

 This heirloom
is meant for greater things
like warming Daniel
while he naps on a snowy day,
unaware that someday
it will belong to him,
and better still his grandchildren
whom I will never know.

What I Want

I want you to find my favorite dress,
the blue silk with long sleeves
that I always wore on special occasions.
I want you to send it to the cleaners
and then give it away.
Don't even think of dressing
what's left of me in it.

I want all of the spare parts,
corneas and kidneys, liver and heart,
to be transplanted like the tulip bulbs
that need to be thinned out each fall
before winter hardens the earth.

I want you to be kind to strangers,
because with all those organs
making music in other people,
you'll just never know
who might be carrying a piece of me.

I want you to place my ashes
in the tea tin I keep on my kitchen counter,
the one with the picture
of two cardinals in the snow.
Do not buy an urn.
They tend to be ugly
and far too expensive.

I want you to use the money
you would have spent
on the ugly urn
for a plane ticket to Ireland
and find the apple tree in Killarney
where we scattered
Nanny Marge's ashes
when you were eighteen.

I want you to find a nice B&B
near the cemetery at Aghadoe
where our guide led us to the tree,
leaving the entire tour group

to fend for themselves
while he found the perfect spot
to deposit the dearly departed.

I want you to remember
how he stood at a respectful distance
uttering a quiet prayer
while we poured the ashes
around the tree
twenty paces to the right
of John Cronin's headstone.

I want you to find John Cronin's headstone
and pause under the tree
and memorize every detail of the place—
grass rolling down to the water's edge,
weathered Celtic Crosses blanketed with moss,
watery light piercing the clouds
over the islands dotting the lake.

That's what I want…

But if all that seems a bit too elaborate,
just find a lovely tree and
pour out all that's left.
That's what I really want after all,
to be poured out,
to nourish the soil,
to let nothing go to waste.

Wisdom Quilt

I believe "we convince by our presence."[1]
I believe "a foolish consistency is the hobgoblin of little minds,"[2]
And " it's not what you look at that matters, it's what you see,"[3]
I believe "the future lies in the hands of the creatively maladjusted,"[4]
And that "faith is taking the first step even when you cannot see the whole staircase."[5]
I believe that "Hope is the thing with feathers/That perches in the soul,"[6]
And I believe "All you need is love."[7]
I believe "you've got to wake up every morning with a smile on your face,
And show the world all the love in your heart."[8]
And I believe, "We shall never know all the good that a simple smile can do."[9]
I believe in "The peace of wild things,"[10]
And that "happiness really is a warm puppy."[11]
I believe in the "poems and prayers and promises,"[12]
Of those who have gone before me.
I believe "All sorrows can be borne if you can put them into a story,"[13]
And "there is no greater agony than bearing an untold story inside you."[14]
I believe in stitching together the fabric of other people's wisdom
and wrapping myself in the quilt of their insights to find out who I am.
I believe I am the offspring of Walt Whitman and Maya Angelou,
Ralph Waldo Emerson, Isak Dinesen, and John Denver,
Martin Luther King, Carol King, Wendell Berry, the Beatles,
Emily Dickinson, Stephen Sondheim, Snoopy, Mother Teresa,
and my own mother who said,
"Go write a story."[15]

---

[1] Walt Whitman
[2] Ralph Waldo Emerson
[3] Henry David Thoreau
[4] Martin Luther King, Jr.
[5] Martin Luther King, Jr.
[6] Emily Dickinsen
[7] John Lennon
[8] Carol King
[9] Mother Teresa
[10] Wendell Berry
[11] Charles Schultz
[12] John Denver
[13] Isak Dinesen
[14] Maya Angelou
[15] Margaret Cahill

When **Gloria Heffernan** was six years old, her mother told her, "Go write a story." She has been writing ever since. In the past five years she has focused most of her creative energy on writing and teaching poetry.

At the age of 55, Gloria retired from a thirty-year career as a higher education and non-profit administrator, to turn her attention to writing full-time. Her decision was fueled in part by her wonderful experiences in the creative writing classes at Le Moyne College in Syracuse, New York, where she studied with Linda Pennisi, Patrick Lawler, and David Lloyd. She is grateful for their encouragement and guidance as she took their classes with eager and talented undergraduates who both inspired and intimidated her.

Listening to the bravery, creativity and enthusiasm of these young writers motivated Gloria to launch her own community-based poetry workshop, "Defying Gravity: Poetry as a Spiritual Practice." She owes a debt of gratitude to Nanncy Slonim-Aronie, whose book and workshop, *Writing from the Heart* was a turning point in both her writing and her teaching.

Gloria has published poems and short stories in over forty literary journals including *Chautauqua, Comstock Review, Columbia Review, Gargoyle, Jabberwock, Louisville Review, Stone Canoe, The Healing Muse, The Wayfarer* and *Written River*.

Gloria is an adjunct instructor in critical writing at Le Moyne College. She holds a Masters degree in English from New York University. She lives in Syracuse, New York, with her husband, Jim Heffernan, and their dog, Maxwell.

Some of Our Parts is her first chapbook. Her first full-length volume, entitled *What the Gratitude List Said to the Bucket List* will be published by New York Quarterly Books in 2019.

www.ingramcontent.com/pod-product-compliance
Lightning Source LLC
LaVergne TN
LVHW041557070426
835507LV00011B/1141